Biographies of famous people to support

First published in 1996
by Franklin Watts
This edition 2002

Franklin Watts
96 Leonard Street
London EC2A 4XD

Franklin Watts Australia
56 O'Riordan Street
Alexandria, Sydney
NSW 2015

ISBN 0 7496 4358 7 (pbk)

A CIP catalogue record for this book is available from the British Library

Dewey Decimal Classification
Number: 942.01

10 9 8 7 6 5 4 3 2 1

Series Editor: Sarah Ridley
Designer: Kirstie Billingham
Consultant: David Wray & Dr. Anne Millard

Printed in Great Britain

Alfred the Great

Long ago, the people of England were called Saxons. They lived in four kingdoms: East Anglia, Mercia, Northumberland and Wessex.

Alfred was born in 849. He was the youngest son of the King of Wessex, and grew into a clever child.

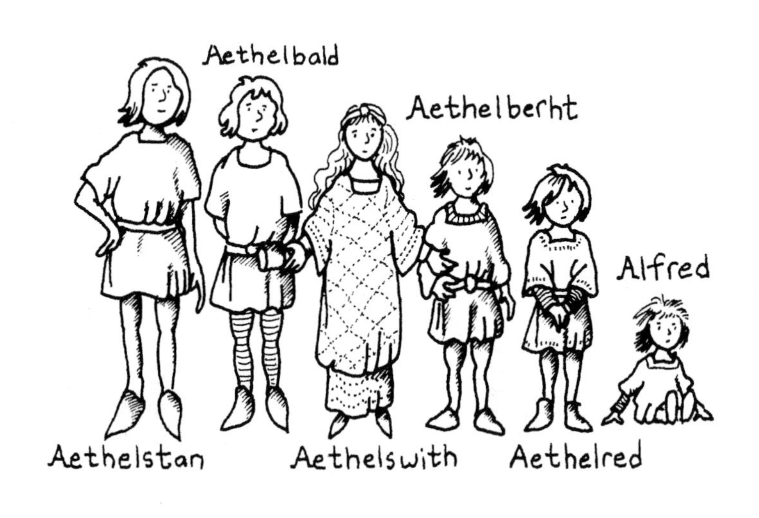

When he was four, his father took him on a journey to Rome, where he met the Pope. The people of Rome were interested in painting, music and learning.

The young Alfred must have been impressed. What he saw there may have given him ideas for the future.

Once his mother showed a beautiful book to her children.

"I will give this to the one who can read it to me first," she said.

Alfred could not read so he took the book to his teacher. The teacher read the book out loud until Alfred knew it all by heart.

He won the prize.

Alfred was born in troubled times. The Vikings had come across to England from Denmark in their longships. They were not Christians like the Saxons, but worshipped their own god, Odin.

The Vikings wanted the rich lands of the Saxons, so they made war. The Vikings were fierce fighters and won battle after battle.

The Saxons were worried.

When Alfred was twenty-one, a Viking army marched into Wessex. Aethelred, Alfred's older brother, was king at the time. He took his Saxon soldiers to a place called Ashdown to fight the Vikings.

There he waited with Alfred.

When the Vikings came,
Aethelred was busy praying.
It was Alfred who led the Saxons into battle, charging towards the enemy, swinging his sword.

The Vikings were taken by surprise, and they were beaten.

But there were other battles.
The Vikings won every one.

Aethelred fell ill and died.
The Saxons made brave young
Alfred their king.

Alfred and his men fought the Vikings at the Battle of Wilton, but lost. They had to make peace and gave the Vikings gold. The Vikings promised not to make war on Wessex again.

But the Vikings did not mean to keep their promise.

In the winter of 877, Alfred, who was twenty-eight by now, went to his fort at Chippenham for a Christmas feast. Twelve days

later, the Vikings came with a huge army. The Vikings knew the Saxons would be feasting and would not be ready to fight.

The Vikings killed many people and burned their homes. They captured the fort at Chippenham, but they could not find Alfred.

Alfred has gone. Curse him!

Alfred had escaped with some of his men. They went from place to place, begging for food and shelter from the cold.

After many weeks, they reached Athelney. Athelney was an island in the middle of the Somerset marshes. There was a building on the island that they could use as a fort to hide from the Vikings.

A story is told of Alfred at this time. It says that Alfred stayed for a few days with a farmer and his wife. They did not know he was the King.

One morning, the farmer's wife spoke to Alfred.

"I must milk the cows," she said. "Watch those oat cakes cooking on the fire. Don't let them burn."

But Alfred was thinking about how to fight the Vikings. He forgot all about the cakes and they burned. When the farmer's wife came back, the room was full of smoke.

"You foolish good-for-nothing!" she shouted. "You can't even look after a few cakes!"

She was so angry that she hit Alfred over the head with a broom.

When spring came, Alfred sent messages to all the Earls in Wessex so that they would know where he was.

At Easter, Alfred heard the great news that the Earl of Devon had beaten a Viking army in battle.

Good news at last!

Alfred knew it was time to stop hiding. He rode through Wessex and met his Earls and their soldiers at a place called Egbert's Stone.

The Saxons cheered Alfred for some had thought he was dead. When they saw him, hope filled their hearts.

The Viking army, led by Guthrun, was at Edington, not far away. Alfred and the Earls made battle plans and prayed all night.

Next morning, the Saxons marched to Edington and the battle began.

The Saxons stood close together.
Their shields made a wall to
keep back the Vikings.
The fighting went on all day.

Arrows flew through the air.
The ground was red with blood,
but at last, the Vikings turned
and ran.

Alfred chased the Vikings to the fort at Chippenham. The Saxon army camped around the fort and waited.

After two weeks the Vikings gave up. They thought that Alfred would kill them, but instead, Alfred made peace.

It was agreed that the north and east of England belonged to the Vikings. It became known as 'the Danelaw' because Danish law was used there. Wessex and the south belonged to the Saxons.

Guthrun had to convert to Christianity.

Alfred made Wessex strong. He built walls round many towns so that people could take cover if the Vikings attacked.

He built a navy of fine, fast ships that beat the Danish navy in battle in 875.

In 886, Alfred went to live in London. He put up new buildings and London grew into a rich city.

Alfred made new laws. He rewrote books from the Latin language into Saxon, so that more of his people could learn from them.

The Saxons loved their king for all the good things he did. They called him 'Alfred the Great'.

Alfred died in 899 at the age of fifty. His son, Edward, became King. Alfred's grandson, King Athelstan, won the last battle against the Vikings in 937.

When Edgar, Alfred's great-grandson became King, he ruled over Saxons and Vikings. He was the first king of all England.

N

Further facts

The Vikings came from Denmark and Norway. As well as being great sailors and fearsome fighters, they were poets, artists, explorers and traders. They spread all over Europe and settled in Iceland and North America.

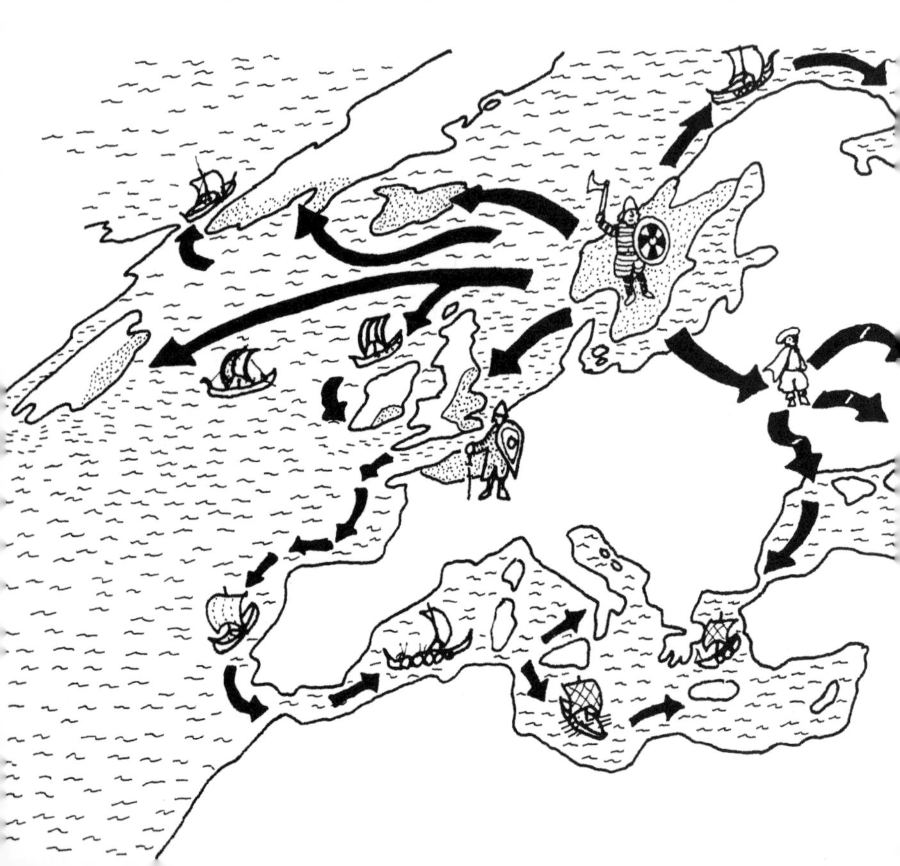

Despite the threat from the Vikings, Alfred found time to encourage interest in writing, reading, music and art amongst his people.

Alfred founded what eventually became the Royal Navy. The ships he ordered to be built were good enough to beat the Vikings in a battle at sea. Up until then, people had believed that Viking ships were invincible.

In 1693, a jewel was found near Athelney. It is a rock crystal, set in gold, showing a man, possibly Alfred himself. There are letters in Latin which read 'Alfred ordered me to be made'. The jewel is called 'The Alfred Jewel'.

Some important dates around Alfred's lifetime

793	Viking raids on England begin.
842	The Vikings attack London.
849	Alfred is born.
865	The Vikings take over East Anglia.
870	The Battle of Ashdown. The Saxons beat the Vikings.
870	The Vikings take over Northumberland.
871	Alfred is crowned king and the Saxons lose the Battle of Wilton against the Vikings.
874	The Vikings take over Mercia.
878	The Vikings attack the Saxons at Chippenham. Alfred goes into hiding. Battle of Edington — Saxons victorious. Peace with the Vikings.
886	Alfred goes to live in London.
886	The Vikings attack Paris.
892	The Vikings return but Alfred is prepared and beats them with a good army and navy.
896	Alfred and his army drive the Vikings out after four years of fighting.
899	Alfred dies.
937	Alfred's grandson, King Athelstan, wins the last battle against the Vikings in England.
959	King Edgar, Alfred's great-grandson, becomes the first king of all England.